PATAGONIA TRAVEL GUIDE
2022/2023

Written by locals

Featuring Ushuaia, Torres del Paine, El Calafate & El Chaltén

Bartolomé, Gerardo
Patagonia Travel Guide: 2022-2023 / Gerardo Bartolomé; photos by Paula Ford.
1st edition - Buenos Aires, Argentina, Ediciones Históricas, 2022.
128 p.; 20 x 14 cm.

ISBN 9798848725278

Cover by Paula Ford and Gerardo Bartolomé.
Book design by Ricardo Dorr.

Table of Contents

Introduction
Planning a trip to Patagonia?

Welcome to our Patagonia Travel Guide. This book will be very helpful for you to understand what is there to see and do and specifically how to plan your trip so that Patagonia fulfills everything that you expect from your holidays and more.

Paula and I live in Argentina and have travelled through this fascinating region for more than thirty years, writing books and photographing amazing places. We now want to share all our "local knowledge" to help you improve the holidays that you want to spend here. Our goal is that your amazing trip to Patagonia starts with a great planning experience.

This guide does not describe in depth all of Patagonia for we have focused on the places that can make a most powerful impact on travellers coming from overseas. There is so much to see! But time is not infinite… so we have focused on chosen places and activities rather than making a long list with which you would feel lost. According to this strategy we offer you selected places in Patagonia, which, depending on how much time you have, can be visited in the same trip. We will suggest different alternatives for shorter or longer visits.

As you read you will find links (or QRs to scan) that will take you to immersive 360° photos where you will be able to explore and understand many places. Some of these 360° photos have icons which you can click to go from place to place or to see more information. We think that this 360°-technology can be very helpful and gives you an extra value.

Feel free to write to us asking for more information, suggestions, or doubts. Our email is Consultas@EdicionesHistoricas.com.ar

Once again: Welcome to our Patagonia Travel Guide.

PAULA & GERARDO

Chapter 1
What you need to know to plan your trip, and some helpful tips

1.1 Getting started

Patagonia is so big and there's so many different things to see that probably you don't know how to start planning your trip. Don't worry! We'll help you and you'll start enjoying Patagonia right from the planning experience.

Since distances are great you won't be able to have a good taste of this region if your visit is short. In fact, a short visit can be a frustrating experience. We say that you should come no less than two weeks, much better if it is three weeks. Remember that Buenos Aires or Santiago de Chile are, necessarily, part of the trip, so you should spend two or three days there too.

Since Patagonia is a region shared by two countries, Argentina and Chile, it is important that you find out if they demand you a visa or charge you with some entry fee (depending on your nationality). Once you find that out, and the costs involved, you'll be able to decide whether to cross the border between both countries or stick to only one.

1.2 How to visit Patagonia?

You can join a tour, you can travel on your own in a fully self-planned trip, you can combine both or you can seek guidance and pre-booking from Travel Agencies dedicated to incoming tourism.

English is spoken in touristic destinations but hardly when you leave the main towns. This means that moving with a rented car, or with public transportation, might be a bit challenging for those

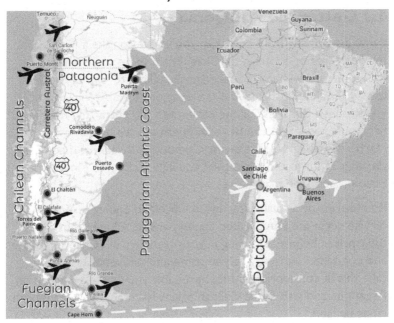

who don't speak or understand a word of Spanish. Don't take this as a final objection but consider it when you plan your trip (or parts of your trip). Other languages than English or Portuguese are not spoken at all, even in important cities, except in hotels or cruise ships.

If you decide to rent a car keep in mind that you should always try to have your gasoline tank full because distances are long and sometimes gas stations are closed. Try to avoid driving at night, guanacos cross the roads unexpectedly causing accidents.

Use weather apps or websites (Windguru or Meteored) to check the ever-changing Patagonian weather.

1.3 Getting to Patagonia

If you are coming from overseas, you'll have to take a flight to Buenos Aires or Santiago de Chile. From there to southern Patagonia you will have to take another flight to one of these towns: Calafate, Ushuaia, Río Gallegos or Punta Arenas. If you want to visit the coast or the mountains of central and northern Patagonia your flight can be from Buenos Aires to Bariloche, San Martín de los Andes, Trelew or Comodoro Rivadavia. If coming through Santiago the Chile then you'll fly to Puerto Montt or Pucon (check the map above).

Round trips by airplane starting in Chile and ending in Argentina or vice versa are complicated and expensive. Check flights and their prices before advancing in your planning. In "Chapter 7: Ideas and combinations" we give you some alternatives that already take this in consideration. Most probably you'll base your trip on Argentina and visit some Chilean places from nearby Argentinean cities by land.

1.4 When

We recommend southern hemisphere's summer (winter in northern hemisphere) not only because Patagonia is a cold region but also because days are very long in summer. November through April would be good and better if you avoid the high season of January and February. Exceptions to the rule are if you want to ski or enjoy whale watching.

1.5 What to do

Patagonia is a fantastic place for enjoying incredible views and landscapes as well as for performing outdoor activities. Local food and drinks are also interesting; don't expect fancy restaurants but

WILDLIFE OBSERVATION CHART

Species	Summer Jan - March	Fall April - June	Winter July - Sept	Spring Oct - Dec	Where	
Whales	O	-	+	-	C	O None
Penguins	+	-	O	+	C	- Few
Sea lions	+	-	-	+	C	+ Many
Elephant seals	+	-	-	+	C	
Orcas / Killer whales	-	-	-	-	C	C Coast
Guanacos	+	+	+	+	C - S	S Steppe
Foxes	+	+	+	+	C - S - A	A Andes
Pumas	-	-	-	-	S - A	
Choique / Patagonian rhea	+	+	+	+	C - S	
Cormorants	+	+	-	+	C	
Dolphins	+	+	+	+	C	
Swans	+	+	-	+	C - S - A	
Geese	+	+	-	+	C - S - A	
Flamingos	+	+	-	+	C - S - A	
Other Sea birds	+	+	-	+	C	
Other Forest / Steppe birds	+	+	-	+	C - S - A	

rather old fashioned "bodegones" (half way between an English pub and an Italian cantina). Don't expect either to do a lot of shopping in Patagonia except for some souvenir-buying. Leave shopping for Buenos Aires or Santiago de Chile.

When we say "outdoors activity" we mean mostly trekking, bird watching, wildlife observation, photography and simply enjoying awesome places like glaciers, mountain ranges, lakes with incredible colours and endless forests, all this can be visited by foot, car, bus or boat. Patagonia offers amazing experiences for all nature lovers.

Patagonia Virtual Tour

1.6 Budget

Holidays in Patagonia can be planned to be low budget if you have time to use public transportation and to camp or to sleep in hostels. If you plan your trip using plane, tour, guides, 4-5 star hotels, then your budget will be similar to that of a trip to Australia, New Zealand, Canada or USA since, in Patagonia, prices are set in US dollars. But you can get around this if you pay cash in pesos and change your foreign currencies in places where you can get a superior exchange rate. This is a very important issue that must be considered because it will make a lot of difference. Feel free to write to us about this since economic conditions might change.

1.7 Our rating system, stars and other tags

We use stars and tags to make it easy for you to understand and separate what you want to do or see. Here are the criteria that we used to rate.

Stars for destinations

*** – Means that you must or should go – A destination where you can spend 3 days or more with unforgettable activities/experiences.

** – Means that you should consider visiting – A destination where you can spend 1 or 2 days with unforgettable experiences.

* – Means that a short detour is worthwhile – A destination where there is at least 1 great or unforgettable activity/experience.

No star, only mention – Means that if you pass by and have time, there could be an interesting activity/experience

Stars for activities/experiences

*** – Means that if you like certain type of activity/experience (like trekking or birdwatching, etc) then you must/should do this one because it is unforgettable.

** – Means that if you like certain type of activity/experience then you should consider doing this one because it is amazing or remarkable.

* – Means that if you like certain type of activity/experience and have time +budget, then this one can be interesting.

No star, only mention – Means that if you have extra time, this activity/experience can be interesting.

Physical Intensity – Used to classify trekking and other outdoors activities.

Intensity 3 – An activity for people fit and energetic. Similar to jogging 10 km.

Intensity 2 – An activity for people moderately fit. Similar to jogging 5 km.

Intensity 1 – An activity for people that can walk 5 km.

Intensity 0 – No special physical ability required other than walking 500 mts on flat ground.

Cost – This tag is only an indication, not a quotation and is related to the duration of the activity.

High Cost – A full day activity over 150 US dollars per person or 75 if half day or 50 if 2 or 3 hours.

Medium Cost – A full day activity around 75 US dollars per person or 40 if half day or 25 if 2 or 3 hours.

Low Cost – A full day activity below 50 US dollars per person or 30 if half day or less than 15 if 2 or 3 hours.

Scenic – Used to classify the beauty of a landscape.

Scenic 3 – Awesome. You must see it.

Scenic 2 – Great place. You should see it.

Scenic 1 – Nice. Try to see it.

Photography – Used to classify the possibility of taking great pictures. Could be landscape, wildlife, monuments, buildings or situations.

Photography 3 – Awesome. Could be the cover of a magazine.

Photography 2 – Great to post in your social networks.

Photography 1 – Nice. Try to go back home with that picture.

Wildlife – Used to classify the quantity and opportunity to observe wildlife.

Wildlife 3 – Great opportunity (almost certain) to observe many, different and impressive animals.

Wildlife 2 – Opportunity to observe various animal species.

Wildlife 1 – Possibility to observe some animal species.

Duration of the activity

Multi day

Full day

Half day

2-3 hours

Chapter 2
Ushuaia

2.1 Introduction

Southernmost city in the world[1], Gate to Antarctica, End of the World, this city deserves all these titles.

Great views of the mountain ranges, lots of things to do and the feeling that you really are in a remote location make Ushuaia a "must" in your trip to Patagonia. Plan no less than 3 full days and better if it is 5 or 6.

---

1. This title is challenged by the Chilean town of Puerto William, but it is disputable whether Puerto Williams is truly a city or a village.

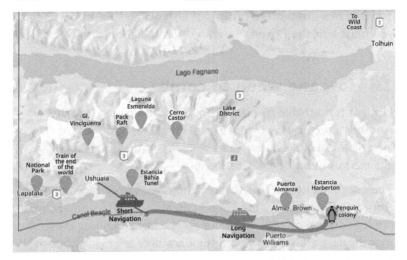

Ushuaia offers a great deal of activities whether you prefer physical effort, simple sightseeing, wildlife observation or if you are interested in history.

2.2 A bit of history

Home of the Yaghans and visited by *HMS Beagle* with Darwin on board, this region was disputed by Argentina and Chile during most the XIXth century. In 1870 an Anglican preacher, Thomas Bridges, founded here a mission which attracted Yaghans and Selknams escaping from the growing animosity of settlers, which were encouraged by the government. In 1884 Argentina moved Bridges to create here a settlement and so Ushuaia was born.

In 1902 a prison was built receiving dangerous prisoners from all over the country and so the small town started to grow providing services to the prison. The city became the capital of the (Argentine) Territory of Tierra del Fuego which achieved the status of province in 1990. Since then, tourism has given Ushuaia an incredible impulse to economic and population growth.

To learn more about the history of Ushuaia and Tierra del Fuego you must visit the Prison Museum (Museo Marítimo).

2.3 How and when to come

Ushuaia is reachable by plane from Buenos Aires or Calafate. Another alternative is by boat from Punta Arenas onboard the incredible Australis cruise ships while navigating the Fuegian channels as described in Chapter 6.

The best time of the year to come here goes from November to April (mostly summer) but keep in mind that January and February are high season months so prices will be higher. During these months days are very long and temperatures are mild although mornings can be cold.

Ushuaia is also very visited during June through October because of winter sports. If you are thinking of coming during northern hemisphere's summer (winter in Ushuaia) keep in mind that weather is very cold, and few activities are recommended other than skiing.

2.4 Where to stay

There are great, and expensive, hotels in Ushuaia. Many are located high over the town, with incredible views overlooking the Beagle channel and the mountain ranges of Navarino Island. We can name a few: Las Hayas, Los Acebos and Arakur. Another recommended hotel is Los Cauquenes Resort & Spa, this one by the coast of the Beagle channel. There are many other hotels within the town although not as striking as the mentioned ones.

A great alternative for travelers is to rent an apartment (use typical well-known websites) many of which have nice views of the harbor and mountains.

Feel free to write to us regarding this issue. We'll be happy to help you.

2.5 What and where to eat

Ushuaia has a great number of restaurants. On the main street (San Martín) you'll be able to find old looking pioneer houses offering old fashioned food like stews or soups. What's special in this city is the Fuegian lamb and seafood, specially eating king crab. On the way to Glaciar Martial there is a tea house/restaurant that serves Swiss cheese fondue. For excellent cuisine and great views over the channel go to the restaurant of Hotel Arakur. Regarding eating king crab, consider visiting Puerto Almanza (separate explanation ahead) to have an unforgettable experience.

2.6 Moving around

Most of the activities that you'll hire include transfer, but you might want to visit some places on your own. In that case you can either rent a car (don't leave it for the last moment), buy van transfer tickets (near the harbor entrance) to/from main places or take a taxi (you can call it using whatsapp).

2.7 What to do

Ushuaia is a place where you can find excellent activities both active (like trekking) or passive (like visiting places onboard boats, vans, or buses). That means that here people of all ages and physical fitness can have a great time. We have listed and grouped most of the available activities and commented them.

ACTIVITY RATINGS - USHUAIA

Activity	Rating	Intensity	Scenic	Duration	Cost	Photography	Wildlife
Short Beagle Navigation	**	0	2	Half Day	Med	2	2
Long Beagle Navigation	***	0	2	Full Day	High	3	2
Train End of the World	*	0	1	Half Day	Med	1	1
Tierra del Fuego Nat. Park	***	0 to 2	1	Full Day	Low	2	2
Pack Raft	**	1	2	Half Day	Med	2	1
Lake District	**	0	2	Full Day	High	2	1
Lake District & Wild Coast	***	0	3	2 Days	High	3	2
Helicopter Ride	***	0	3	2 Hours	High	3	0
Estancia Harberton	**	0	1	2 Days	High	2	1
Penguin colony	**	0	1	2 Hours	Med	3	2
Puerto Almanza	*	0	1	2 Hours	Med	1	0
Prison Museum	*	0	0	2 Hours	Low	1	0
Hop on Hop off	*	0	2	3 Hours	Low	2	1
Walking the city	*	1	1	2 Hours	Low	2	1
Ski in Cerro Castor	**	2	2	Full Day	High	1	0
Trekking	***			Check separate chart			

2.7.1 Short Beagle Channel Navigation **

It is one of the most popular activities in Ushuaia. The boat leaves from the pier in Ushuaia and navigates the islands in front of the harbor with great views of the city and the mountain range behind it. Then the boat will sail towards the East (with great views on both sides) until it reaches Les Eclaireurs lighthouse which is one of the most photographed spots in Tierra del Fuego. During the navigation sea lions, cormorants, seagulls and other sea birds can be spotted.

Tags: 2 Stars – Intensity 0 – Scenic 2 – Half day – Medium Cost – Photography 2 - Wildlife 2.

2.7.2 Long Beagle Channel Navigation + Harberton + Penguins ***

This is a great alternative for those who will not be staying long in the area. It combines the previous navigation but goes further East to visit the historic Estancia (Ranch) Harberton and a penguin colony that includes two different species (see below further detail on both activities). Check weather forecast before hiring the trip because weather makes a lot of difference. Get ready for a long day with many things to see and do.

Tags: 3 Stars – Intensity 0 – Scenic 2– Full day – High Cost – Photography 3- Wildlife 2.

2.7.3 Train of the End of the World *

It is one of the most popular activities in Ushuaia. The train leaves from a station, in the surroundings of Ushuaia, that can be reached by taxi. It goes along the old track used to take prisoners who were forced to log trees for firewood for the prison. The trip ends in a station in the National Park, but the hiking paths and other nearby interesting places are not near the station so, to visit the park you must either walk a lot or combine (with a local agency) the train with a bus. The old locomotives and wagons have been painted and refitted in a remarkable way. The tracks run along a scenic way with nice views of the forest and the mountains. The entrance fee to the park is not included in the ticket.

Tags: 1 Star – Intensity 0 – Scenic 1– Half day – Medium Cost – Photography 1 – Wildlife 1.

2.7.4 Tierra del Fuego National Park ***

A "must" when you visit Ushuaia, this National Park protects a large area that goes from the coast to the inner mountain ranges,

including lakes and glaciers. It is home to dense forest, dozens of birds as well as other animal species. It can be visited in a passive way (in a tour or rented car) or can be walked, since it has a great number of trekking paths like the coastal path (9 km) or many others going up into the mountains (more detail in the "trekking" section of this chapter). You must pre-arrange your transport options within the park since there is no public transport and no mobile phone signal to call a taxi. Alternatives are, rented car, the train (although you'll still need transport within the park) pre-arranged taxi or van transfer service (with a timetable in different places of the park).

Tags: 3 Stars – Intensity 0 to 2 according to your choice – Scenic 1– Full day – Low Cost – Photography 2 – Wildlife 2.

2.7.5 Pack Raft down Olivia River **

This is certainly an incredible experience. The deal is to float down the winding river Olivia for approximately two hours on an individual boat called pack raft, similar to a kayak but much more stable. The transfer van will take the group 15 km from Ushuaia. There the guide will give to each person a backpack with the inflatable boat inside. The group will then walk for 45 minutes to a lagoon where the boats will be inflated. Everyone will receive instructions and practice rowing movements on the lagoon. Then the group will start the floating experience. The river runs, quietly, through a marshy area with great views of the surrounding mountains while enjoying this fabulous experience.

Tags: 2 Stars – Intensity 1 – Scenic 2– Half day – Medium Cost – Photography 2 – Wildlife 1.

2.7.6 Trekking ***

Ushuaia (and surroundings) is one of the most amazing places for trekking in all of South America. Here you will find alternatives with different intensities, views and landscapes. Since the places are not within walking distance of the city, you'll need to buy a van transfer ticket (way and back) or you can arrange with a taxi, or you can rent a car (taxi is cheaper than car rental). Here goes a list, and brief description, of the trekking alternatives that we recommend most:

TREKKING RATINGS - USHUAIA

Trekking path	Rating	Intensity	Scenic	Duration	Cost	Photography	Wildlife
Coastal Path in National Park	**	1	2	Full Day	Low	1	1
Laguna Esmeralda	**	2	2	Half Day	Low	2	1
Ojo del Albino	***	3+	3	Full Day	Med	3	1
Glaciar Vinciguerra	**	3	1	Full Day	Med	2	1
Glaciar Martial	*	2	2	Half Day	Med	2	0
Estancia Túnel & Río Encajonado	**	1	2	Half Day	Low	2	1

2.7.6.1 Coastal Path in National Park **

Beautiful hike mostly through the forest along the coast of the Beagle Channel. Aprox 3 to 4 hours (9 km). Low trekking intensity. Bird photography as well as great views of the mountains of the southern coast of the channel.

Tags: 2 stars – Intensity 1 - Scenic 2 – Half day – Low Cost – Photography 1 – Wildlife 1.

National Park coastal path

2.7.6.2 Laguna Esmeralda (Emerald Lagoon) **

Amazing hike to a lagoon formed by glacial water 200 mt above the starting level. Initially the path leads you through the forest which then becomes a steep rocky slope. Medium trekking intensity, 10 km (way and back), 4 to 5 hours. The starting point is 20 km from the city. Transfer with van or taxi (no cell phone signal so arrange to be picked up). Entrance is free. Tip: go in the morning, once by the lagoon, walk around it (1.5 km) to really enjoy the place. Some people join a group with a guide, although it is not needed.

Tags: 2 stars – Intensity 2 - Scenic 2 – Half day – Low Cost – Photography 2 – Wildlife 1.

Laguna Esmeralda

2.7.6.3 Ojo del Albino ***

Incredible and difficult walk to a high lagoon (800 mt above starting point) where a glacier calves with floating icebergs. The way is basically the same as to Laguna Esmeralda but goes beyond it. Very high trekking intensity, 21 km (way and back). A guide is necessary for this hike which provides the transfer to and from the hotel.

Tags: 3 stars – Intensity 3+ - Scenic 3 – Full day – Medium Cost – Photography 3 – Wildlife 1.

2.7.6.4 Glaciar (Glacier) Vinciguerra **

Amazing and difficult hike to a glacier including a walk on the ice itself (14 km, 700 mt above starting point). The walk starts with a steep hike through the forest. Although not mandatory, the hike should be done with a guided group. The guide will provide you with the crampons required to walk on ice plus he will take charge of the transfer from the hotel to the starting point and back.

Tags: 2 stars – Intensity 3 - Scenic 1 – Full day – Medium Cost – Photography 2.

Glaciar Vinciguerra

2.7.6.5 Glaciar (Glacier) Martial *
Very near the town, this is a good alternative to hike to a glacier (4 hrs, 250 mts above starting point) with great views over the

city and Beagle Channel. The way is not very easy to find, and some parts are quite steep, so it is better if you join a guided group which will also provide you with transfer.

Tags: 1 star – Intensity 2 - Scenic 2 – Half day – Medium Cost – Photography 2.

2.7.6.6 Estancia Bahía Túnel & Río Encajonado **

Nice and easy walk along the Beagle channel East of the city. The starting point is a coastal beacon where the dust road ends about 10 km from the town center. You can walk until an abandoned ranch by the sea (Estancia Bahía Túnel) and come back or you may continue to Río Encajonado, according to your energy. The distance (way and back) is 6 km/3 hrs or 10 km/5 hrs, depending on where you turn back. The path goes along the coast with great views of the channel and the mountain range of Navarino island and has many short but steep parts. The best way to go to the starting point is taking a taxi and arranging the pickup time.

Tags: 2 stars – Intensity 1 - Scenic 2 – Half day – Low Cost – Photography 2.

Estancia Bahía Túnel

2.7.6.7 Other trekking alternatives

Mount Susana, Laguna Turquesa, Cerro Alerkén, Hito and Cerro Guanaco (both in National Park). For those who want more adventure, there are other alternatives like crossing the mountain ranges and camping for 2 to 3 days (with a hired guide).

2.7.7 Lake District **

Take a tour on 4x4 vehicles to cross the mountain range on the north of Ushuaia. Beyond it lie several lakes surrounded by a dense forest. Eventually the forest recedes becoming a steppe where the guanacos live. The Garibaldi Pass viewpoint will leave you speechless and from there the vehicles will drive through rough dirt roads towards Lago Escondido (Hidden lake) and Fagnano.

Tags: 2 stars – Intensity 0 – Scenic 2 – Full day – High Cost – Photography 2 – Wildlife 1.

2.7.8 Lake District and Wild Coast ***

This alternative is 2 days long. It includes the previous tour but instead of heading back to Ushuaia on the same day it continues

north-east to sleep in domes placed on the Fuegian steppe, home of the Patagonian guanaco. The wild Eastern coast is then explored including Cape San Pablo and a stranded ship on an endless beach.

Tags: 3 stars – Intensity 0 – Scenic 3 – 2 Full days – High Cost – Photography 3 – Wildlife 2.

Wild Coast

2.7.9 Helicopter Ride ✳✳✳

Ushuaia offers helicopter rides over many different areas, always with incredible views of the city, the Beagle channel, the mountain ranges, lagoons, glaciers and much more. The ride is not cheap but, certainly, you will remember it as one of the top activities in Patagonia. Different circuits (with different prices) can be chosen. Although the flight time is 20-30 minutes, consider 2 hours as the total time including transfer, waiting time, security explanation, etc.

Tags: 3 stars – Intensity 0 – Scenic 3 – 2 Hours – High Cost – Photography 3.

2.7.10 Estancia Harberton **

70 km east of Ushuaia, connected by a dust road, lies the most historic place of Tierra del Fuego. Harberton belongs to the descendants of Thomas Bridges, the missionary and first European settler of the island. The ranch house was constructed on a peninsula by the Beagle channel with its own harbor. All the materials to build the house were brought from England (in the 1880s) and assembled where it lies today. The place certainly keeps the pioneers' atmosphere. Recently a very interesting exhibition of sea life was installed in one of the old buildings. Even though the place can be visited as a day trip, we recommend staying one night to really feel the peace and freedom of being away from everything. Tours can hired, or you can rent a car to go there. A short visit to the ranch is included in the Long Beagle Channel Navigation (including the penguin colony).

Tags: 2 stars – Intensity 0 – Scenic 1 – 1 or 2 Full days – High Cost – Photography 2 – Wildlife 1.

Estancia Harberton

2.7.11 Penguin Colony **

If your trip to Patagonia is planned mainly to mountain areas (such as Calafate, El Chaltén or Torres del Paine) then this will be your only chance of seeing a penguin colony. Tens of thousands of jackass or Magellanic penguins nest in Martillo (Hammer) Island, near Harberton. On the same island also nest about forty couples of Gentoo penguins (usually nesting in Antarctica), it is the only place on the continent that they do so. Sometimes also a couple of King penguins can be seen. Following your guide's advice, you'll be able to walk among the penguins and take unforgettable pictures. The island is also home to other interesting bird species such as steamer ducks, skuas and seagulls, to name a few. To visit the place, you can take de Long Beagle Channel Navigation or you can book a visit through Harberton (if you sleep there).

Tags: 2 stars – Intensity 0 – Scenic 1 – 2 hours visit – Medium Cost – Photography 3 – Wildlife 2.

2.7.12 Puerto Almanza *

This quiet little fishermen's village 60 km east of Ushuaia is home to several seafood restaurants. The best alternative is to plan to have lunch here on your way to/from Harberton. Some tours stop here but usually only as a bus stop to take pictures, missing the lunch opportunity. The restaurants in Almanza are famous for serving king crab. Having an entire one (to be shared by two people) is quite an experience. Either before or after lunch, you can take a short walk through the woods to a waterfall (40 min) where some nice pictures can be taken.

Tags: 1 star – Intensity 0 – Scenic 1 – 2 hours not including travel time – Medium Cost– Photography 1.

2.7.13 Prison Museum (Museo Marítimo) *

The old prison is home to a very interesting museum featuring the amazing naval history regarding the southern tip of the continent where more than one hundred shipwrecks have occurred. The exhibition is placed in what used to be prison cells preserving the "old prison" atmosphere. The museum is within walking distance from the town's main street and can be visited in a couple of hours. Its visit is a "must" and best if done during the afternoon after the daytime activities.

Tags: 1 star – Intensity 0 – 2 hours – Low Cost – Photography 1.

Prison Museum

2.7.14 Hop on Hop off City Tour *

This is an excellent alternative to get to know the town and have

its history explained. The double decker leaves from the city center and takes about 3 hours for the round trip. Lots of nice pictures to be taken!

Tags: 1 star – Intensity 0 – Scenic 2 – 2-3 hours – Low Cost – Photography 2 – Wildlife 1.

2.7.15 Walking the city center *

The city center can be visited as a round circuit. Walk ten blocks along San Martín Street and come back by the coast avenue (Maipú). Some shopping can be done, and you'll also have a chance to take some nice pictures. Look for old pioneers' houses, souvenir and outdoors equipment shops and nice old looking restaurants but you'll also have a chance to have some great views of the Beagle channel, see a stranded ship and do some birdwatching. Include a visit to the garden below the government house.

Tags: 1 star – Intensity 1 – Scenic 1 – 2 hours – Low Cost – Photography 2 – Wildlife 1.

Walking the city center

2.7.16 Ski and other winter activities **

Most of the activities described above are possible during winter but keep in mind that weather can be very harsh and ice can cover trekking paths plus days are very short. But the city offers ski fans from the northern hemisphere, the possibility to practice this sport and other winter activities when ski centers in Europe and USA/Canada are closed for summer. Cerro Castor (20 km from Ushuaia) is a big ski center with guaranteed snow for many months. Other winter activities besides skiing or snowboarding are: dogsled rides, snowmobile, snowshoeing, off road 4x4 tours and much more.

2.8 Some ideas and suggestions

People have different budgets, different interests and more or less time to spend here. But considering that you might feel lost with so many alternatives, here go some ideas as to what to do according to how much time you'll stay in Ushuaia.

2.8.1 If staying 3 days

We recommend:

Long navigation of Beagle Channel including Harberton and penguin colony.

End of the World Train to visit Tierra del Fuego National Park, maybe including part of the coastal trekking.

According to your interests and energy choose one of the following:

Low physical intensity: Lake district in 4x4.

Medium/High intensity: Pack-raft or Trekking to Laguna Esmeralda or Vinciguerra glacier.

Use your free time during the afternoon for a Hop-on Hop-off city tour and visit the "Museo Marítimo" in the old prison building.

2.8.2 If staying 7 days or more

We recommend:

Short navigation of the Beagle Channel.

Rent a car for a couple of days and visit on your own: Harberton, sleeping there. Puerto Almanza. Penguin colony. National Park maybe including coastal trekking. Pack rafting in Olivia River.

Trekking, 1 or 2 circuits, according to your interest and energy: Laguna Esmeralda. Glaciar Vinciguerra. Bahía Túnel – Río Encajonado.

Lake District & Wild coast – 2 days.

Use your free time during the afternoon for a Hop-on Hop-off city tour and visit the "Museo Marítimo" in the old prison building.

Helicopter ride.

Chapter 3
El Calafate

3.1 Introduction

Visiting Calafate means seeing the Perito Moreno glacier, certainly one of the most awe-inspiring places of Patagonia and maybe the most spectacular glacier in the world. If you come to Patagonia then you must see the Perito Moreno and so Calafate becomes a mandatory stop in your holidays. But there are other things to do in the area to make your stop here a very pleasant stay.

The city lies by the side of Lake Argentino whose fjords reach into the Andes. The water of the lake has milky blue color caused by tiny rock particles (called rock flour) grinded by the many glaciers of the area. Calafate is the gate to the immense Parque Nacional los Glaciares, translated as Glaciers National Park. The city's horizon is shaped by the mountains, home of a giant ice field that separates Argentina from Chile, the third largest mass of ice in the world, behind Antarctica and Greenland.

The area is rich in history of explorers (like Darwin and Moreno) and pioneers from all around the world.

Plan at least 2 days if you are only interested in seeing the Perito Moreno, but it is much better if you stay 4 or 5 days to really enjoy the place.

Most of the activities in Calafate don't demand physical effort, so you'll be able to save your energy for your visit to El Chaltén.

3.2 A bit of history

The Patagonian steppe was home of Tehuelches tribes, the legendary Patagonians named by Magellan. They lived mainly of the hunt of the guanaco and benefitted greatly of the introduction of horses, mainly escaped or taken from Spanish settlements.

Following the expeditions of Darwin/FitzRoy (1834) and later, that of Francisco Moreno (1877), European settlers arrived and established their ranches along the Santa Cruz River up to Lake Argentino. The price of wool produced an important economic growth. In 1927 the town of El Calafate was founded to provide a commercial hub to the settlers.

In 1937 the area was included in the creation of the Glaciares National Park but it wasn't until the decline of the price of wool, in the 1960s, that the Perito Moreno glacier was viewed as a touristic opportunity and, from then on, El Calafate received an enormous economic impulse.

3.3 How and when to go

Calafate is reachable by plane from Buenos Aires or Ushuaia. It is connected by land to Torres del Paine (Chile) with a 5 hour drive (or bus), and not far from El Chaltén (2 hours away by van or car).

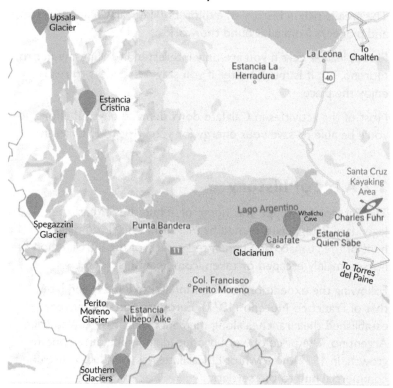

The best time of the year for coming here goes from November to April (mostly summer) but keep in mind that January and February are high season months so prices will be higher. During these months days are very long and temperatures are mild although mornings can be cold.

3.4 Where to stay

There are many hotels in Calafate that go from five stars to hostels for backpackers, so you shouldn't have trouble in finding one that suits your budget. They are mostly located inside the urban area and mostly within walking distance from the town's center. There are a couple of fancy "estancias" that offer lodging, but they are far away from the town so keep that in mind if you choose that alternative.

Feel free to write to us regarding this issue. We'll be happy to help you.

3.5 What and where to eat

Calafate has several restaurants on the main street (San Martín). Most of them offer Patagonian lamb on the grill but you'll also be able to find Italian food like pizza and pasta. Many pubs where beer and fast food is served can be found on the main street.

3.6 Moving around

Almost all of the activities that you'll hire include transfer. To visit the national park, including the Perito Moreno (which is 80 km away from the town), you can take a tour but you can also rent a car and do it on your own. You might save a little money if you rent a car (it only makes sense if you also use that car to visit El Chaltén) but keep in mind that it is not necessary, usually the activities are far away from the town and include transfer service.

3.7 What to do

Most of the activities in Calafate don't require physical effort (there are a couple of exceptions). That means that, no matter what your age is, here you can have a great time. We have listed and grouped most of the available activities and commented them.

ACTIVITY RATINGS - EL CALAFATE

Activity	Rating	Intensity	Scenic	Duration	Cost	Photography	Wildlife
Perito Moreno Glacier - walkways	***	0	3	Half Day	Med	3	1
Ice mini-trekking + walkways	***	1	3	Full Day	High	3	0
Short navigation + walkways	***	0	3	Full Day	Med	3	0
Estancia Cristina + Upsala	**	0 to 2	3	Full Day	High	3	0
Estancia Cristina + Upsala - 2 days	***	0 to 2	3	2 Days	High	3	1
Long Nav. to Gl. Upsala + Spegazzini	**	0 to 1	2	Full Day	Med	3	0
Estancia Nibepo Aike full day	*	1	1	Full Day	Med	2	1
Estancia Nibepo Aike 2 days	**	0 to 2	2	2 Days	High	2	1
Estancia Nibepo Aike + PM Gl.	***	1	3	Full Day	High	3	1
Southern Gl. + Nibepo Aike	**	1	3	Full Day	High	3	1
Kayaking Santa Cruz River	**	1	1	Half Day	Med	2	1
Glaciarium - Ice Museum	*	0	0	2 Hours	Low	1	0
Walichu cave	**	1	1	3 Hours	Med	2	1
Laguna Nimez	*	1	1	2 Hours	Low	2	2
Day trip to El Chaltén	**	1	3	Full Day	Med	3	1
Walk City Center	-	0	0	2 Hours	Low	1	0

3.7.1 Perito Moreno Glacier (walkways) ***

Definitely a big "must" when coming to Patagonia. You will never forget the front of this huge glacier and you might as well remain hours watching and waiting for big pieces of ice to fall to the water with a thunder-like sound from as much as 60 meters high. A bus (or van) will take you across 50 km of steppe and 30 km of progressively greener environment, pay attention for you might see condors on the way. From the parking lot you'll find the way to a series of walkways at different levels and angles where you'll have awe inspiring views of the front of this massive wall of cobalt blue ice. Not a bit short of amazingly incredible. You can stay up to two hours simply staring in awe, but you can also complement this passive experience with one of the following activities (described separately): mini-trekking on ice, short navigation of lateral wall or Nibepo Aike ranch. Even though it is an awesome place, if you only go to the walkways you'll have the feeling that you missed something.

Tags: 3 Stars – Intensity 0 – Scenic 3 – Half day – Medium Cost – Photography 3 – Wildlife 1.

Perito Moreno Walkways

3.7.2 Mini trekking on ice + Perito Moreno walkways ***

A great combination for an unforgettable day but, unfortunately, only allowed for people under 65. This activity must be booked in Calafate at least one day in advance. It includes transfer and visit to the front walkways (explained before). From a small pier, less than 1 km south of the walkways you will board a boat that will take you to the other side of the lake. During those 15 minutes you will sail parallel to the southern front of the ice with amazing views. Once landed on the other side the group will walk (slight slope) for half an hour till the border of the glacier where everyone will receive crampons to walk on the ice. For one hour you'll walk over the glacier, between towers of ice and deep blue pools; an amazing experience that ends with a toast of whisky with glacial ice.

Tags: 3 Stars – Intensity 1 – Scenic 3 – Full day – High Cost – Photography 3 – Wildlife 1.

Mini ice trekking

3.7.3 Short navigation + Perito Moreno walkways ***

A great combination but just a little short in excitement when compared to the mini-trekking. This activity must be booked in Calafate at least one day in advance. It includes transfer and visit to the front walkways (explained before). From a small pier, less than 1 km north of the walkways you will board a boat that will take you navigating the northern wall of the glacier about 70 meters tall. Guides will explain past and present of the Perito Moreno while you keep taking pictures of the wall of ice.

Tags: 3 Stars – Intensity 0 – Scenic 3 – Full day – Medium Cost – Photography 3 – Wildlife 1.

3.7.4 Navigation to Estancia Cristina + Uppsala Glacier **

Lake Argentino is enormous. One of its fjords is home to another massive glacier named after the Swedish city of Uppsala. Not far from it an English pioneer first settled in the area, more than 100 years ago, creating what now is Estancia Cristina. There are two alternatives to visit this fantastic place, full day visit or staying there for 1 or 2 nights. The full day alternative starts at a pier 40 km west of Calafate (transfer included) and 2 hours navigation to the Uppsala Fjord where dozens of icebergs, some as big as the boat, float making you feel in Antarctica. Then the boat will take you to Estancia Cristina where you have a menu of activities: visit the Pioneers Museum, 4x4 drive to the Uppsala viewpoint, have an "asado" for lunch or hike from the Uppsala viewpoint to the main house (14 km). You'll have to choose between the asado and the hike (includes lunch box). By midafternoon the group will board the boat back to Calafate while you'll regret not having booked a night there.

Tags: 2 Stars – Intensity 0 or 2 if trekking – Scenic 3– Full day – High Cost – Photography 3.

Iceberg during navigation to Upsala glacier

3.7.5 Navigation to Est. Cristina + Uppsala glacier + lodging ✳✳✳

Similar to the previous alternative but if you choose to sleep in Estancia Cristina you'll find time and peace to truly enjoy this corner of the world. Rooms are spacious and sunny, lunch and dinner are quiet and superb, and you will be able to choose more activities from the menu, like: horse riding, fly fishing, birdwatching, hiking, guided tour of the ranch, photography and much more. At least one night will make a lot of difference,

but you can also stay 2 or 3 nights. It's all a matter of time and budget.

Tags: 3 Stars – Intensity 0 or 2 if trekking – Scenic 3 – 2 days – High Cost – Photography 3 – Wildlife 1.

Estancia Cristina Virtual Tour

3.7.6 Long Navigation to Glaciers Upsala & Spegazzini **

It is a full day trip navigating the northwestern fjords of lake Argentino. You will observe the glaciers at a certain distance with the Andes mountains as a background and dozens of floating icebergs. A short walk is optional.

Tags: 2 Stars – Intensity 0 – Scenic 2 – Full day – High Cost – Photography 2 – Wildlife 0.

3.7.7 Estancia Nibepo Aike full day program *

This estancia has kept the pioneer's architecture and is located in a fantastic place, near the lake and great views to the mountain ranges. It offers several activities such as: horse riding, hiking, sheep shearing, old ranch guided tour as well as lunch (including local asado). Why "only" 1 star? Because the full day program brings so many people to the ranch that the place loses part of its "old pioneers" atmosphere. Fortunately, Nibepo Aike offers other programs.

*Tags:1 Star – Intensity 0 – Scenic 1 – Full day – Medium Price –
Photography 2 – Wildlife 1.*

Nibepo Aike Outdoors

3.7.8 Estancia Nibepo Aike 2 days program **

Similar to the previous alternative but, as the "full day program"
visitors leave, you'll find yourself in a peaceful quiet place, home of
the pioneers that settled the area. The rooms, which retain all of the
"old days" spirit are really something you will enjoy and photograph!
With more time you will be able to profit from the activities offered
by the ranch, such as: horse riding or hiking over the hills behind the
ranch from which the Perito Moreno can be seen and, if you reach
the summit, Torres del Paine will also be visible.

*Tags: 2 Stars – Intensity 0 or 2 if trekking or horse riding – Scenic
2 – 2 days – High Cost – Photography 2 – Wildlife 1.*

Nibepo Aike Room

3.7.9 Estancia Nibepo Aike + Perito Moreno ***

This alternative combines a short visit to the ranch (including lunch) with a spectacular visit to the glacier. You'll board a boat that will take you to the pristine far (western) side of the lake. There the group will do a short walk through the forest to a place with views of the side of the Perito Moreno. You will board again to navigate along the impressive southern wall of ice to land on the eastern side. A van will be there to take you to the walkways in front of the glacier, as previously described. Since it will be afternoon, the place will be almost deserted which makes it even more attractive. After around one hour the van will take you back to Calafate. Although the day will be a bit rushed it will be remembered as one of the best of your vacations. You can also arrange to sleep in Nibepo Aike and, the following day, join the Perito Moreno option.

Tags: 3 Stars – Intensity 1 – Scenic 3 – Full day – High Cost – Photography 3 – Wildlife 1.

Nibepo Aike Walk to glacier

3.7.10 Southern glaciers + Nibepo Aike **

The "Glaciares National Park" is home to many more impressive glaciers and this magnificent tour will let you see massive ice formations that only few see. The day starts leaving Calafate very early in the morning when a van will take you to Nibepo Aike. After a very short visit to the ranch, you will board a boat to navigate to the southern end of the lake where the group will be landed. After a short walk to lake Frias, the group will board another boat to take you further South, almost to the border with Chile where, in a natural amphitheater three glaciers are seen. A truly amazing trip. You can also arrange to sleep in NIbepo Aike and do Southern glaciers the day after. This tour is not offered every day so be sure to check dates in advance.

Tags: 2 Stars – Intensity 1 – Scenic 3 – Full day – High Cost – Photography 3 – Wildlife 1.

3.7.11 Kayaking the Santa Cruz River **

Darwin and FitzRoy explored the Santa Cruz River from the Atlantic to about 20 km east of the lake, which they never saw and missed discovering. You can have a bit of the flavor of that

expedition by kayaking down the river and discover that it hasn't almost changed since 1834. For two hours you'll float down the milky blue river together with guides who will take care of all the safety measures necessary to have an excellent experience. The trip ends with a lunch by the side of the river.

Tags: 2 Stars – Intensity 1 – Scenic 1 – Half day – Medium Cost – Photography 2 – Wildlife 1.

3.7.12 Glaciarium or Ice Museum *

It is located 5 km from Calafate and has a shuttle bus that connects, for free, this museum with the town. The visit will take about 2 hours. The outside of the building will call your attention and inside it there is an outstanding exhibition explaining to you past and present of this region, shaped by the growing and contracting masses of ice. It's a good idea to visit Glaciarium in the afternoon after a half day activity and prior to dinner.

Tags: 1 Star – Intensity 0 – Scenic 0 – 2 Hours – Low Cost – Photography 1.

3.7.13 Walichu cave **

This activity is different from anything that you might expect in Calafate. The group leaves Calafate onboard Land Rover Defenders. Few km from the town the off-road track will start through the desert-like steppe around Calafate. In Punta Walichu you'll have excellent views of the lake and the mountains and the sun falling behind it all. Walichu means Devil in Tehuelche language. The place has this name because the explorer Moreno found here an old Indian mummy. The rocky walls have dozens of archeological paintings as much as 8.000 years old, meaning that the place was inhabited when the ice fields still covered a large part of lake Argentino. The visit ends with a dinner in a cave (Walichu cave) covered with these paintings.

Tags: 2 Stars – Intensity 1– Scenic 1 – 2 to 3 Hours – Medium Cost – Photography 2 – Wildlife 1.

3.7.14 Birdwatching in Laguna Nimez *

The shallow coast of the lake, within the city limits of El Calafate, is the nesting area of dozens of different bird species. Part of it is protected as a reserve called Laguna Nimez. Flamingos, black necked swans, Patagonian geese, ducks, egrets, coots, snipers and many others can be seen just a few feet away as you walk around this wetland. Paradise for birdwatchers! Although it is within walking distance from the city center, you should take a taxi and maybe save your energy to walk back to town.

Tags: 1 Star – Intensity 1 – Scenic 1 – 2 Hours – Low Cost – Photography 2 – Wildlife 2.

3.7.15 Day trip to El Chaltén **

Yes, El Chaltén can be visited from Calafate as a full day tour, but we strongly recommend not to unless you have decided not to spend there the 3 or 4 days that it really deserves. As a day tour you'll be able to see the incredible FitzRoy granite massif named after Darwin's captain. Best places for nice pictures are the lookout 3 km before entering the town or Parques Nacionales' building right before the village. Recommendable: a short walk to the Chorrillo waterfall and a visit to the first pioneer's house (Madsen) turned into a small museum. Depending on your fitness there is a short but steep walk to the Cóndor lookout where there is an incredible view of the village and surrounding area. Either going or returning you should stop by Parador La Leona, an

old house turned into a pioneer's pub with a small museum-like exhibition. Have a coffee and buy yourself an "alfajor"or "torta frita". You'll have a long great day, but you'll return to Calafate a bit frustrated as you'll understand how much you have missed by not staying a few days in El Chaltén.

Tags: 2 Star – Intensity 1 – Scenic 3 – Full day – Medium – Photography 3.

3.7.16 Walking the city center

The city center doesn't have much of interest except that you can do some souvenir shopping and choose a restaurant for your dinner. All the activity is located on eight blocks along the main street (San Martín). You may visit the garden of Parques Nacionales where you'll find statues of Moreno and Darwin, among others.

Tags: No star – Intensity 0 – Scenic 0 – 2 hours – Low Cost – Photography 1.

3.8 Some ideas and suggestions

People have different budgets, different interests and more or less time to spend here. But considering that you might feel lost with so many alternatives, here go some ideas as to what to do according to how much time you'll stay in Calafate.

3.8.1 If staying 2 full days

We recommend:

Perito Moreno Glacier; walkways combined with either mini-trekking or short lateral navigation.

Choose one of these two: Navigation to Estancia Cristina + Uppsala glacier. Nibepo Aike and Southern glaciers

If you are returning to Calafate up to 5pm and still have energy, try to pay a visit to Glaciarium.

3.8.2 If staying 4 days or more

We recommend:

Perito Moreno Glacier; walkways combined with: Mini-trekking. Short lateral navigation. Nibepo Aike + navigation.

Choose one of the following: Estancia Cristina + Uppsala either full day or 2 days options. Nibepo Aike (1 or 2 days) + Southern glaciers.

Walichu Cave or Kayaking in Santa Cruz River.

Birdwatching in Laguna Nimez.

Glaciarium.

Chapter 4
El Chaltén

4.1 Introduction

This little village is considered the trekking capital of Argentina. The hills behind it are home to many glacial lagoons, dense forests, glaciers, vertical mountains and, behind it all, an immense ice field 300 km long and 50 km wide.

The town lies on a corner of two rivers: Rio de las Vueltas and FitzRoy. Its background is dominated by two outstanding mountains: FitzRoy and Cerro Torre. Torre means tower, when you see it you'll understand why. These two peaks are among the most challenging in the planet and mountaineers from all over the world come to climb them. We don't expect that much from you, so we'll recommend several trekking paths with different levels of intensity and other activities that don't require that much effort.

If you like trekking, plan about 4 days if not 2 or 3 days will do.

4.2 A bit of history

In 1877 Francisco Moreno explored this area and named Mt FitzRoy after the English captain of *HMS Beagle*. While the area was disputed with Chile the Dane Andreas Madsen was the lone settler a few hundred yards from the nowadays town. In 1984 most of the area was awarded to Argentina, but Lago del Desierto remained disputed. To further ground its territorial claim, Argentina founded the town of El Chaltén in 1985 and finally, in 1994, the border between the two countries was settled.

Mounts FitzRoy and Torre attracted hundreds of professional climbers because of their extreme difficulty. The latter remained undefeated until after Mt Everest was.

In 1937 the area was included in the creation of the Glaciares National Park and in the 1990's the town received a great impulse of tourism which continues today.

4.3 How and when to go

El Chaltén is reachable by plane from Buenos Aires (or Ushuaia) using the airport of Calafate, almost 200 km away. You can come either by van transfer or with rented a car from Calafate.

The best time of the year for coming here goes from November to April (mostly summer) but keep in mind that January and February are high season months so prices will be higher. During these months days are very long and temperatures are mild although mornings can be cold.

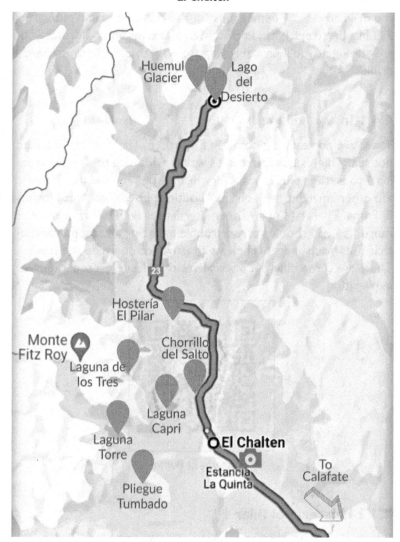

4.4 Where to stay

The village is not more than ten blocks long and 3 blocks wide.
That means that you can go anywhere with a short walk. Although

the main street is Guemes most of the restaurants and pubs are in San Martín street (yes I know... San Martín again) Wherever you are staying at you'll probably want to walk to San Martín to have a drink.

4.4.1 In the village *

There are no really big hotels in El Chaltén. The only big one (and not really big) is Los Cerros. It's walking distance to the pub area, it's 4 to 5 stars, plus it has a very nice restaurant and bar. There are other small but high quality "boutique hotels" such as Hostería El Puma. There are many other alternatives with different price ranges, so you shouldn't have trouble in finding an accommodation that suits your budget. They are mostly located inside the town. There are three different alternatives that deserve a separate explanation.

Hostería El Puma

4.4.2 Hostería el Pilar **

It is a refurnished old house (with wifi!). Very nice, quiet, cozy surrounded by trees and nature. You'd love staying there except that if you don't have a car you'll be stranded because it is 15 km from the town connected by a dust road. This option is very good for hikers because there are several trekking options starting here.

If you'd like to stay here but won't have a car we'd recommend that you book only two days here and for the rest of your stay choose an accommodation in the town. The place requires booking with many weeks in advance, so don't leave it for last minute.

4.4.3 Aguas Arriba Lodge ✳✳✳

This incredible place is as far away from everything as you can be. Here you'll have dinner facing a glacier and you'll have hiking paths and a guide almost for your own. This lodge stands by the coast of Lago (lake) del Desierto, 37 km away from El Chaltén plus a 15 min motorboat ride. Constructed all in wood and glass you'll have light, views, silence, and excellent food. But you'll be almost 2 hours away from El Chaltén, so if you lodge there assume that you are not in El Chaltén. If you want to stay here (you won't regret it) we'd recommend you to also book at least a couple of days in El Chaltén so that both locations complement each other.

Aguas Arriba Lodge

4.4.4 Domes *

There are two domes facilities in the area. One on the other side of the Rio de las Vueltas and the other on the road to Lago del Desierto. Although they are very appealing it is important that you know that, if you don't have a car, you'll be stranded there. So, we'd recommend that if you do want to have that experience, you save some other days to sleep in the town.

Feel free to write to us regarding this issue. We'll be happy to help you.

4.5 What and where to eat

El Chaltén has a number of grill restaurants most of them offer Patagonian lamb, but you'll also be able to find Italian food like pizza and pasta. Many pubs where beer and fast food is served can be found on the main street.

4.6 Moving around

Almost all of the hiking paths start in the village so you can do all right without a car. A car or van is necessary to visit Lago del Desierto and it is helpful (but not absolutely necessary) to visit Madsen's house/museum or to go to Chorrillo del Salto or to Parques Nacionales. Taxis are available to go to some places but, most probably, not to come back because you won't have mobile phone or 4G signal.

4.7 What to do

Most of the activities in El Chaltén are related to trekking and sightseeing and do require some physical effort (but we will list quite a few below that don't). This means that people who are

ACTIVITY RATINGS - EL CHALTÉN

Activity	Rating	Intensity	Scenic	Duration	Cost	Photography	Wildlife
Road from/to Calafate	**	0	2	3 Hours	Low	3	1
Road to Lago del Desierto	**	1	3	Full Day	Med	3	1
Madsen's House Museum	*	0	1	2 Hours	Low	1	0
Kayaking Río de las Vueltas	**	1	2	Half Day	Med	2	0
Wildlife observation	*	1	1	-	Low	2	2
Trekking	***			Check separate chart			

not physically fit will not find El Chaltén as appealing as people who are fit. Anyways, all will agree that the magnificent view of FitzRoy and Cerro Torre is well worth the trip. We have listed and grouped most of the available activities and commented them.

4.7.1 Road to/from Calafate ** – 214 km

Lets start from the beginning. When you come from Calafate be sure to pay attention to a number of photography opportunities and travelling experiences.

KM 20 Guanacos on the road *

Along most of the road you might see guanacos. Specially as you leave the town, near the airport, you can get a nice picture of these animals against a backdrop of snowy mountains.

KM 37 Bridge over Santa Cruz River *

Stop and take a look at this mighty glacial river where it bends in a horseshoe-like curve. Its milky blue color is truly mesmerizing.

Calafate - Chaltén road, bridge over the Santa Cruz River

KM 38 Glacier erratic

On your right you'll see a very big rock. It was drawn by Perito Moreno during his 1877 expedition to this area. It is a glacier erratic and it was left by the retreating ice field that covered all of this area, 20 thousand years ago.

KM 52 La Leona River

The road leaves lago Argentino to border, for the next 50 km, another unforgettable glacial river: La Leona (the lioness), which connects lakes Viedma and Argentino.

KM 106 Parador La Leona *

Stop and have a coffee with alfajor in this old pioneer house turned into a gaucho pub. There is a small historic exhibition, spend a few minutes to see it. The "parador" lies right beside La Leona River, on the spot where Perito Moreno was attacked by a

female puma (a lioness) back in 1877. This is your last chance to take a great picture of the river.

KM 150 Scenic Route 23 to El Chaltén **

For the next 60 km the road runs due West pointing towards Mt FitzRoy. It is usually covered with clouds so when you see it cleared of clouds stop the car (or van) get down and take pictures. Eventually, 3 km before the town there is a lookout with a (similar) spectacular view but, only if the massif is not covered with clouds. So don't take chances, when you see it, shoot your camera!

KM 213 Parques Nacionales Administration house

Stop here to get information regarding trekking paths, weather conditions and wildlife observation. The garden is a great place to take a nice picture of Mt FitzRoy.

Tags: 2 Stars – Intensity 0 – Scenic 2 – Photography 3 – Wildlife 1.

4.7.2 Wildlife observation *

There are no obvious places to admire wildlife in El Chaltén as in other Patagonian places but, if you're alert, you'll certainly will be rewarded. When walking through the forest do it quietly, giving it a chance to hear a distant toc toc of the Patagonian woodpecker, if you do, look for it! Or when in high places, search for flying condors, or check the streams and lagoons for geese, ducks, black necked swans or flamingos. Caracaras (caranchos), chimangos, eagles, hawks and foxes can be seen at any moment. If you like birdwatching, you should be leaving El Chaltén with over 30 species observed.

Tags: 1 Star – Intensity 1 – Scenic 0 – Photography 2 – Wildlife 2.

4.7.3 Trekking ***

El Chaltén is, certainly, one of the most amazing places for trekking in all South America. Here we will give you alternatives with different intensities, views and landscapes with a brief description. Keep in mind that weather here is a bit tricky and that FitzRoy and other mountains are usually covered by clouds coming from ice fields in the west, so when they are visible stop whatever you are doing, admire and take pictures. Best pictures in the morning because the sun, in the East, will lighten the massif. In the afternoon the mountains will be backlighted. So, very simple, for great views of the mountains go out in the morning. We have grouped our favorites but there are many more. None of these require guidance but you might feel more comfortable if, for the long hikes, you join a guided group.

TREKKING RATINGS - EL CHALTÉN

Trekking path	Rating	Intensity	Scenic	Duration	Cost	Photography	Wildlife
Cóndor & Eagle Viewpoints	**	1	2	2 Hours	Low	2	1
Laguna Capri from El Pilar	**	2	2	Half Day	Low	2	1
Laguna de los Tres	***	3	3	Full Day	Low	3	1
Laguna Torre	***	2	3	Full Day	Low	3	1
Pliegue Tumbado	**	3	3	Full Day	Low	2	1
Glaciar Huemul	***	1	2	2 Hours	Low	2	1

4.7.3.1 Cóndor and Eagle viewpoints **

The walk starts near the Parques Nacionales house, that is crossing the bridge out of town, meaning that you have quite a walk to get there. We recommend you taking a taxi to go to Parques Nacionales and leave your energy for the hike and to return walking to the town. A steep but short walk to the top of a hill with great views of the mountain range and, to the North, the valley of the winding Río de las Vueltas coming down from Lago del Desierto. In front of you the village of El Chaltén. Be

alert, condors are to be seen. After admiring the view, take the path to the South and after 15 minutes you will reach the Eagle viewpoint where you will see Lake Viedma, with an intense milky light blue color.

Tags: 2 Stars – Intensity 1 – Scenic 3 – 2 Hours – Low Cost – Photography 2 – Wildlife 1.

Cóndor viewpoint

4.7.3.2 Hostería Pilar + Laguna Capri **
This hiking path is long (4hs) but has no challenging slopes. You'll need a taxi to take you to El Pilar and from there follow the

path by the side of the creek through the forest. Enjoy the nice views and be alert for you might see or hear woodpeckers. You'll eventually pass by a viewpoint over the Piedras Blancas (white stones) glacier. Follow the track to Poincenot campsite and nearby Laguna Capri, excellent spot for opening your lunchbox. Take the way to El Chaltén and try to find the FitzRoy viewpoint (**) and the Magic Waterfall (***). Eventually you'll reach a lookout over Rio de las Vueltas (**) and from there a steep path down back to El Chaltén. You can also do this hike from El Chaltén to El Pilar and so you'll get better light on FitzRoy (if starting in the morning) but you should previously arrange to be picked up because there is no mobile phone signal in El Pilar.

Tags: 2 Stars – Intensity 2 – Scenic 2 – Half day – Low Cost – Photography 2 – Wildlife 1.

Magic Waterfall near Capri

4.7.3.3 Laguna de los Tres ***

This is a very long hike (21 km) with very steep parts (900 mts ascent). The track is basically getting to Capri and from there a steep climb (400 mts high) to the lagoon. You can start the hike either from El Chaltén or from Pilar. If you go from Chaltén, before arriving to Capri, take a very short detour to get to the Magic Waterfall (***) with the morning light on FitzRoy. If you are tired when you get to Poincenot campsite or Capri you should turn back. The final climb is very demanding but getting to the Laguna de los Tres is an incredible experience with an outstanding view (***) of the lagoon and the FitzRoy massif. Clouds might cover this mountain so use weather forecast websites to choose the best day for this hike. Leave the following day for low intensity activities. Some people prefer to do this hike in 2 days. In that case take sleeping bags and backpacks to camp in Poincenot and leave the steep climb and return for the next day. You can rent camping gear in El Chaltén.

Tags: 3 Stars – Intensity 3 – Scenic 3 – Full day – Low Cost – Photography 3 – Wildlife 1.

Laguna de los Tres

4.7.3.4 Laguna Torre ✳✳✳

This is a long hike (19 km) with moderate ascent (400 mts) but the reward is huge. You'll come to a lagoon with icebergs where the Torre glacier calves and behind it: the towering Cerro Torre. The path starts in the town and is mostly through the forest but

in open spaces you will have outstanding views of the mountain range. Although not so challenging as the previous hike it still requires physical fitness. Clouds might cover the mountains so use weather forecast websites to choose the best day for this hike. Leave the next day for low intensity activities.

Tags: 3 Stars – Intensity 2 – Scenic 3 – Full day – Low Cost – Photography 3 – Wildlife 1.

4.7.3.5 Pliegue Tumbado **

Another long hike (21 km) with a constant ascent of 1100 mts to a summit with a marvelous view of all the mountain range including Torre and FitzRoy. The path starts by Parques Nacionales, 2 km from the town (you can call a taxi when you're back). Most of the walk is through a forest (woodpeckers might be seen) that gradually disappears, with a final short but steep ascent of 150 mts to the top where you'll have a 360 view of the area. Clouds might cover the mountains so use weather forecast websites to choose the best day for this hike. Leave the next day for low intensity activities.

Tags: 2 Stars – Intensity 3 – Scenic 3 – Full day – Low Cost – Photography 2 – Wildlife 1.

Pliegue Tumbado

4.7.3.6 Glaciar Huemul ✳✳✳

Short but steep hike to a hanging glacier (Huemul) and a glacial lagoon with an incredible turquoise color and outstanding views. The path starts at the parking lot by Lago del Desierto, 37 km from El Chaltén and follows a stream that flows from the Huemul lagoon through the forest. Even if you're not in good shape you can walk all the way to the lagoon but you'll need to take it slow. The prize is truly rewarding. This hike should be combined with a visit to Lago del Desierto.

Tags: 3 Stars – Intensity 1 – Scenic 2 – 2 Hours – Low Cost – Photography 2 – Wildlife 1.

Laguna Huemul

4.7.3.7 Other trekking alternatives

Loma de las Pizarras (Intensity 3), Reserva los Huemules (Intensity 1 to 3), Piedra del Fraile (Intensity 2), Cagliero + Ice trekking (Intensity 3), Vespignani glacier from Aguas Arriba Lodge (Intensity 2).

4.7.4 The road to the North and Lago del Desierto **

Route 23 passes through El Chaltén and goes 37 km north as a dust road. You'll enjoy every bit of it but you'll need a car or hire a tour. The road goes mostly beside the winding Rio de las Vueltas with great views of the mountain range on the other side. Pay attention because you'll have opportunities to take nice pictures of wildlife (mostly birds) and landscapes. When you come back the sun will be on the other side (golden hour), so you'll have different photo opportunities. Below we will point out some places that you should not miss:

KM 9 Chorrillo del Salto **

Translated as "the creek of the waterfall". You'll have to walk

500 mts from the parking lot to reach a waterfall on a pond surrounded by a forest. A nice challenge to your photography skills. The place can also be reached as a 14 km hike (way and back) from El Chaltén.

KM 19 Laguna Cóndor Viewpoint *

A nice place to stop for birdwatching. Black necked swans, upland geese, flamingos and different duck species are to be seen.

KM 33 Cascade Cañadón Río Toro

Water rapids amid the dense forest.

KM 35 Salto del Anillo

Translated as the Waterfall of the Ring, it is a nice spot for a picture.

KM 37 Glaciar Huemul *** – 37 km

The ascent is explained separately, in the trekking section.

KM 37 Hanging Bridge

Less than 200 mts right (east) of the parking lot you'll see a very photogenic hanging bridge over Rio de las Vueltas.

KM 37 Boat trip **

If you take a tour to Lago del Desierto you might include a boat trip to the northern end, very near the border with Chile. During the navigation you'll have spectacular views of Mt FitzRoy and glaciers Huemul and Vespignani.

Tags: 2 Stars – Intensity 1 – Scenic 3 – Full day – Low or Medium Cost – Photography 3 – Wildlife 1.

4.7.5 Madsen's House Museum

On the opposite side of Río de las Vueltas stands the house that belonged to Andreas Madsen, the first pioneer of the area, in the beginning of the 20th century. It is interesting to understand how harsh life was back in those days. It is 3 km from the town, so if you don't have a car, you can take a taxi and walk your way back. Check opening and closing hours before you go.

Tags: 1 Star – Intensity 0 – Scenic 1 – 2 hours – Low Cost – Photography 1.

4.7.6 Kayaking in Rio de las Vueltas **

This activity can be done even by those who don't have kayak experience. Great views and lots of fun. There are half day and full day alternatives.

Tags: 2 Stars – Intensity 1 – Scenic 2 – Half Day – Medium Cost – Photography 2.

4.7.7 Other activities

Local agencies (like FitzRoy Expeditions) organize different tours and combinations for birdwatchers, fly fishing fans or 2-3 day hiking and camping or rafting in the surrounding area.

4.8 Some ideas and suggestions

People have different budgets, different interests and more or less time to spend here. But considering that you might feel lost with so many alternatives, here go some ideas of "what to do" according to how much time you'll stay in El Chaltén.

4.8.1 If staying 2 full days

We recommend:

Choose one of these trekking alternatives according to trekking energy: Laguna de los Tres. Laguna Torre. El Pilar - Laguna Capri.

Lago del Desierto including Chorrillo del Salto and Glaciar Huemul.

4.8.2 If staying 4 full days or more

We recommend:

Choose two of these full day trekking alternatives according to your trekking energy and leave one day between them: Laguna de los Tres. Laguna Torre. Pliegue Tumbado. El Pilar - Laguna Capri.

Lago del Desierto including Chorrillo del Salto and Glaciar Huemul.

Combine at least 2 of these activities to make a full day: Kayaking, half day option. Hike to Cóndor and Eagle look out. Madsen's Museum.

Chapter 5
Torres del Paine

5.1 Introduction

Torres del Paine is the most iconic mountain range in Chile and in all of Patagonia. Trekking, scenic landscapes, wildlife and photography make this place a "must" when visiting this region. In the maps the massif has an upside-down W shape and you'll be seeing it always from the South. There are two outstanding rock formations: the Cuernos (horns) del Paine and the Torres (towers) del Paine. You'll go back home with dozens of great photos of both. To the west of the formation stands Cerro Paine Grande (Mt Big Paine), less iconic than the other two but still quite impressive.

The many lakes around the massif were formed when the area was covered by the retreating ice field that still separates Argentina from Chile. They have a milky blue color because they receive water from nearby glaciers.

The place offers the possibility of driving around, enjoying of incredible views with little or no effort at all, but you can also

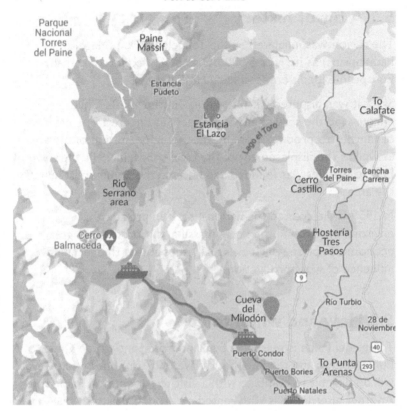

choose short, long and very long trekking paths if you go with enough time and energy.

The accommodation issue is not so easy because there is no town in Torres del Paine. A very small village has developed west of the park (Río Serrano) and the alternative is staying at Puerto Natales, a 90 minutes' drive from the park.

It isn't easy to fit Torres del Paine in a southern Patagonia vacation but believe me that it is well worth the effort.

If you like trekking plan no less than 4 days, if not 3 full days will do.

5.2 A bit of history

The region was inhabited by the Tehuelche tribe (Magellan's Patagonians) as early as 5.000 BC. and was explored by many European expeditions (including *HMS Beagle*).

Since it was disputed with Argentina, in the 1870's Chile encouraged the settlement of pioneers in the area. The creation of ranches to produce wool meant the deforestation of the area as well as the displacement of the local tribes. In 1911 the town of Puerto Natales was founded and became the commercial hub of the area.

In 1959 Chile created the national park to protect the environment around the Paine massif and it produced a great economic impulse which eventually substituted the declining influence of wool production.

5.3 How and when to go

Torres del Paine is reachable by plane from Santiago de Chile to Punta Arenas and then a 4-hour drive (320 km) but in that way it will be difficult to combine with a visit to Argentinian Patagonia. Another alternative is with rented car from Calafate or bus/van Calafate-Pto Natales and there you can hire a tour or rent a car. If you're renting a car in Argentina to cross to Chile (a very good alternative) make sure that the rental company knows that you will cross to Chile because you will have to show a special permit and insurance when crossing the border. Also make sure that you have all the visas and or reciprocity taxes paid (depending on your nationality). It can be a very frustrating experience not to be allowed to cross the border.

The best time of the year for coming here goes from November to April (mostly summer) but keep in mind that January and February are high season months so prices will be higher. During

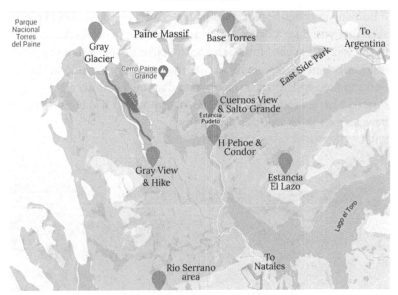

these months days are very long and temperatures are mild although mornings can be cold. March and April have the bonus of forests with red leaves.

5.4 Where to stay

Typically there are two alternatives. Sleeping in the Serrano area, near the west gate of the park, or staying in Puerto Natales but in this case, you'll have a 3-hour drive (90 min way and back) every day. There are other alternatives explained below.

5.4.1 Sleeping in the Serrano area

Alternatives here are expensive and limited, so lodging should be booked well in advance. Consider staying at Hotel Serrano which is very nice, has a good restaurant and great views of the mountains.

If booking in other hotel/cabins (there are 5 or 6 alternatives) make sure that you have a dinner solution for there are no restaurants in the village, except Hotel Serrano. If you're driving a rented car, it is important to keep in mind that there is no gas station in the Serrano area and, most probably, one day you'll have to drive to Puerto Natales to fill your tank, which is not that bad because you'll have an excuse to visit this pretty town.

Río Serrano Area

5.4.2 Sleeping in Puerto Natales

This city has a lot of lodging alternatives that go from 5 stars hotels, like The Singular, to low budget cabins. The town is very nice and offers other interesting places to visit in the sorroundings (like Mylodon's cave) so it is a good alternative but remember that you have quite a drive to the Park.

5.4.3 Within the Park

There are a couple of alternatives in the park with pros and cons.

5.4.3.1 Hotel Explora

It is an excellent alternative if your budget allows it. Luxury and an excellent location.

5.4.3.2 Hotel Pehoe

It has an amazing location with superb views, but very simple rooms.

5.4.4 East of the Park

If you are driving from/to Argentina sleeping near the border is a good alternative to make the most of your first or last day in the Park without driving at night.

5.4.4.1 Cerro Castillo

Less than an hour away from the park, this town has no fancy hotels but for one night it will be all right.

5.4.4.2 Posada Tres Pasos

Almost 2 hours from the east gate of the park, this small hotel is a refurnished old house. It is quiet, retains an "old days" atmosphere combined with good food and great service.

5.5 Moving around

There are two alternatives. Either you have a rented car, in that case you're free to choose whatever you want to do, or you join tours (day or multi day tours) in which case you'll go around with the group to pre-defined places.

5.6 What to do

Almost all that you'll do in Torres del Paine is related to the massif or the lakes around it. It's all outdoors but there are many roads so walking will be a choice, not an obligation.

We have listed and grouped most of the available activities and commented them.

ACTIVITY RATINGS - TORRES DEL PAINE

Activity	Rating	Intensity	Scenic	Duration	Cost	Photography	Wildlife
Salto Grande & Cuernos view	***	1	3	2 Hours	Low	3	0
Lake Pehoe & Cóndor view	***	2	3	2 Hours	Low	3	0
East side Park	**	0	3	Half Day	Low	3	2
Trekking to Base Torres	***	3	3	Full Day	Med	3	1
Navigation to Glaciar Grey	**	0	2	Half Day	Med	2	1
Lake Grey & short hike	*	1	1	2 Hours	Low	2	1
Visit to Puerto Natales	**	0	2	Half Day	Low	2	2
Milodon Cave	*	0	1	2 Hours	Low	1	0
Nav. to Balmaceda & Serrano Gl.	***	0	3	Full Day	High	2	0
Horse Riding El Lazo	**	1	3	Half Day	Med	2	1

5.6.1 Salto Grande waterfall and Cuernos' viewpoint ***

Easy and spectacular walk. The waterfall connects lake Nordenskjold with Pehoe, both share the same milky light blue. Park the car and enjoy 15/20 minutes by the waterfall and then start a walk to the north. In 20 minutes, you'll come by an arm of the lake with an outstanding view of the Cuernos. When the wind stops (if it does) the Cuernos/Horns will be reflected, chance for a great photo. Continue walking for another 20 minutes to the true Cuernos lookout, on the way you'll pass several burnt trees with photogenic shapes.

Tags: 3 Stars – Intensity 1 – Scenic 3 – 2 Hours – Low cost – Photography 3.

Cuernos Viewpoint

5.6.2 Lake Pehoe and Cóndor Viewpoint ✳✳✳

From the lake shore you'll have a fabulous view of Paine Grande mountain and the Cuernos, with a neat contrast between the milky blue waters and the white ice of the mountains. A long bridge connects the Hostería Pehoe with the mainland. Park your car and have a coffee in the Hostería with a grand view of the massif. On the way back, there are seats on the bridge where you can take cool selfies with the mountains as your background. If you have energy for a short but steep walk, hike to the top of the Cóndor viewpoint (40 min hike). From the summit you'll have a spectacular view of the lake, the bridge, the island and the Cuernos.

Tags: 3 Stars – Intensity 2 – Scenic 3 – 2 Hours – Low cost – Photography 3.

Cóndor Viewpoint

5.6.3 East side of the Park **

Drive to the eastern gate of the park along a tremendously scenic road. Be alert because you'll probably see guanacos, foxes and birds.

On your way stop in the following places:

5.6.3.1 Nordenskjold's viewpoint **

Amazing view of the lake and behind it the massif and its impressive towers.

5.6.3.2 Rio Paine waterfall **

A cascade of milky waters with the backdrop of the towers. You might see foxes around.

5.6.3.3 Bridge over Rio Paine *

Short detour to the old bridge that points directly to the towers. A great opportunity for nice pictures.

5.6.3.4 Lagoon/Laguna Amarga *

Cross the gate towards the east. You'll probably see guanacos beside the road. Not far you'll come to a lake where flamingos usually rest. You can't get near the shore but with a good zoom you should be able to take great pictures of the pink animals in the blue lake. Very rarely pumas are to be seen.

Tags: 1 Star – Intensity 0 – Scenic 1 – Half or Full Day – Low cost – Photography 2 – Wildlife 2.

5.6.4 Trekking to Base Torres ***

Long and fantastic hike only recommendable for those who are physically very fit. Although not necessary we suggest joining a guided group. The path goes along the very narrow eastern valley into the heart of the Paine formation. The way goes up continuously and the last 500 mts, over a rocky glacial moraine, are very steep. Finally, you'll arrive to the border of a glacial lagoon with a magnificent view of the three Paine towers. Save energy for the way back. The total distance is 20 km and total ascent is 700 mts.

Tags: 3 Stars – Intensity 3 – Scenic 3 – Full Day – Low/Medium cost – Photography 3 – Wildlife 1.

5.6.5 Navigation to Grey glacier **

A great glacier calves in Lake Grey. The best way to see the 30 mt tall ice wall from a short distance is with the navigation tour which is usually booked in Puerto Natales. A great experience, similar to the navigation in Calafate. Navigation can also include mini-trekking over the glacier. If you have a rented car, consider combining this tour with the short hike on the southern end of the lake.

Tags: 2 Stars – Intensity 0 – Scenic 2 – Half Day – Medium cost – Photography 2 – Wildlife 1.

5.6.6 Lake Grey and trekking *

The southern end of Lake Grey has a rocky beach where floating icebergs are usually brought by the wind. To get there cross the hanging bridge near the parking area and walk for about 15 minutes. Once on the beach, in the distance you'll see the glacier. Continue walking to the eastern end of the beach and then follow the trekking path at the foot of the rocky hill. A 30-minute walk will take you to a view point where you'll see the distant glacier. You can return to the beach following a different foot path that will take you through a forest where woodpeckers and other birds are usually seen. Many people combine this hike with the navigation to the glacier.

Tags: 1 Star – Intensity 1 – Scenic 1 – 2 hours – Low cost – Photography 2 – Wildlife 1.

5.6.7 Other activities in the Park **

Kayaking in Lake Grey or Rio Serrano.

Camping and trekking around the Paine massif, a 4 - 5 days experience.

5.6.8 Other Activities out of the Park ***

5.6.8.1 Visit to Puerto Natales **
This small town by the coast of Seno de Ultima Esperanza (Last Hope Sound) offers great views of the snowy mountains on the other side of the bay. Birdwatching is a must on this coast. Just park by the sea side and you'll be able to see dozens of different species and take great pictures. You must visit the little handicraft market called Etherh Aike. Make sure to see the street art on a wall along street Bernardo Phillipi, depicting the history and culture of the tribes of the area. Last, but not least, if you like seafood don't lose the opportunity of having dinner or lunch in a local restaurant.

Tags: 2 Star – Intensity 0 – Scenic 2 – Half day – Low cost – Photography 2 – Wildlife 2.

5.6.8.2 Milodon Cave *

In 1896 the fur of an extinct giant sloth (called Milodon) was found in a cave. It looked so fresh that many thought the species still roamed the area. The cave is a truly remarkable place, and it is well worth the short detour from the Puerto Natales-Paine road.

Tags: 1 Star – Intensity 0 – Scenic 1 – 2 hours – Low cost – Photography 1 – Wildlife 0.

5.6.8.3 Navigation to Balmaceda and Serrano Glaciers ***

The ice field that separates Argentina and Chile has a number of glaciers that reach into the Pacific Ocean at the end of long fjords. From Puerto Natales you can take a full day boat tour navigating the Seno de Ultima Esperanza that will take you to the front of these two glaciers.

Tags: 3 Stars – Intensity 0 – Scenic 3 – Full day – High cost – Photography 2 – Wildlife 0.

5.6.8.4 Horse riding in Estancia El Lazo **

About one hour from the Park, on the way to the border with Argentina, is this ranch that has an extraordinary view of the Paine massif. It offers horse riding for beginners through forests and up to hill tops with superb views of the lake and mountains behind it. Book in advance with an agency of Puerto Natales.

Tags: 2 Stars – Intensity 1 – Scenic 3 – Half Day – Medium cost – Photography 2 – Wildlife 1.

5.7 Some ideas and suggestions

People have different budgets, different interests and more or less time to spend here. But considering that you might feel lost with so many alternatives, here go some ideas as to what to do according to how much time you'll stay in the Torres del Paine area.

5.7.1 If staying 3 full days

We recommend:

Choose one of these full day activities: Trekking to the Base of the Torres. Navigation in Lake Grey, if possible, combine it with the short hike on the southern end of the lake.

A great scenic day including: Salto Grande waterfall, Cuernos viewpoint, Lake Pehoe, Nordenskjold viewpoint, Río Paine waterfall and Laguna Amarga.

Since you'll need to refuel the car you should visit Puerto Natales and take the detour to Milodon Cave.

5.7.2 If staying 5 full days or more

We recommend:

Navigation in Lake Grey combined with the short hike on the southern end of the lake.

A great scenic day including: Salto Grande waterfall, Cuernos' viewpoint, Lake Pehoe and hike to Cóndor viewpoint.

Choose one of these full day activities: Trekking to the Base of the Torres. Navigation to Balmaceda and Serrano glaciers.

Since you'll need to refuel the car you should visit Puerto Natales and take the detour to Milodon Cave.

Whether you're leaving the area back to Argentina or from Puerto Natales-Punta Arenas you can enjoy a full day by doing the following: East side of the Park including Nordenskjold viewpoint, Río Paine waterfall, bridge over Río Paine and Laguna Amarga. Horse ride in Estancia El Lazo. Sleep in Posada Tres Pasos, enjoy the house and walk the surroundings.

Chapter 6
Other Awesome Places in Patagonia

6.1 Introduction

Patagonia is much more than the previously described four fantastic places (El Calafate, El Chaltén, Torres del Paine and Ushuaia) but time is not infinite (neither is the budget) so we focused on these places that can be combined in the same trip, same time of the year, can be connected with logical transport alternatives and they have many things to do and see. But this planning guide would not be complete if we did not describe and comment other awesome places and let you decide. The description will not be as detailed and intense as the Big Four but we will give you a good idea of what to expect in all these other awesome places.

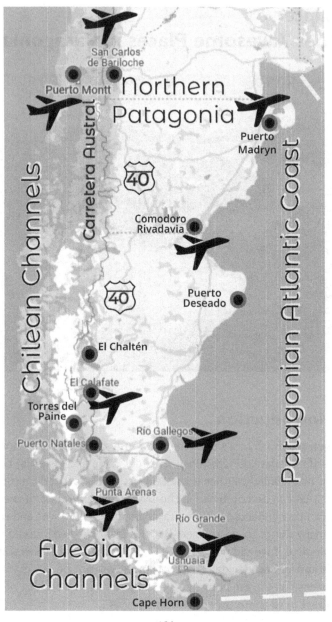

In the near future we will publish guides focusing on these other Patagonian jewels.

6.2 Patagonian Atlantic Coast ***

If you like observing and photographing wildlife this alternative will make sense to you. Year round there are different species to be seen, mostly sea birds, sea mammals and land (steppe) species.

The bad side is that even though there are airports in this area (Puerto Madryn, Trelew and Comodoro Rivadavia) few or no flights connect it with Calafate or Ushuaia. There's always the possibility of doing it passing by Buenos Aires but that means time and money.

6.2.1 Valdes Peninsula ***

This is, probably, the best place for whale watching (***) in the world. Although better if during July and August, you can still see them till November. During summer you can combine a day in the beach (sunny but with cold water) with a tour around the peninsula (**) and see Magellanic penguin colonies, sea-lions and elephant seals as well as guanacos, choiques (Patagonian rhea), flamingos, orcas and dolphins to name a few animals. You can stay in Puerto Madryn with a 90-minutes transfer to the peninsula or you can sleep in the small village of Puerto Pirámides.

We recommend between 3 and 5 days including a visit to these nearby places:

(**) Snorkelling with sea lions in Puerto Madryn.

(*) Gaiman – Visit this old Welsh colony. Have a Welsh tea there and visit some Welsh chapels Half a day.

(*) Dinosaur museum of Trelew. Patagonia used to be inhabited by these giants more than 65 million years ago. This museum has a very interesting exhibition about this subject. 2 hours.

(**) Punta Tombo – a huge Magellanic penguin colony 180 km south of Puerto Madryn.

Dolphins in Rawson – During summer, from the harbor of this small town you can take a motor boat tour to see dolphins, specially the pretty and friendly Commerson's dolphin. 2 hours.

Puerto Pirámides – Valdés Península

6.2.2 Camarones + Cabo Dos Bahías **

This small town "off the beaten track" is like travelling to old Patagonia. The nearby reserve is home of a big Magellanic penguin colony and many other animal species.

6.2.3 Bahía Bustamante ***

It is a privately owned very small village exclusive for tourists where every small house was refurnished keeping its old atmosphere. The place offers tours with well-trained guides. Everybody working to provide an unforgettable stay.

What is there to see? A wild coast with white sandy beaches (but cold water) and many marine animals like Magellanic penguins, sea-lions, skuas and cormorants but also steppe animals like guanacos, foxes and choiques. Not far you can also visit the remnants of a petrified forest.

The whole atmosphere of the place together with tourists from around the world makes this a very interesting experience.

The best way to come here is by plane to Comodoro Rivadavia and have a transfer arranged to Bahía Bustamante (60 km).

We recommend no less than two full days and up to four, depending of time and budget.

Bahía Bustamante

6.2.4 Puerto Deseado ***

This small town has come to be known as the Galapagos of Patagonia because of its numerous and varied wildlife. The bad thing is that the closest airport (Comodoro Rivadavia) is almost 300 km away so, either you pre-arrange a transfer or make a reservation to rent a car in Comodoro Rivadavia's airport.

Plan no less than two days, better if three.

Once in Puerto Deseado the main activities are:

6.2.4.1 Penguin Island ***

It is an almost full day tour to this open-sea island. There you'll see both Magellanic and Rock Hopper penguins but also

cormorants, sea-lions, elephant seals, dolphins, skuas and sea gulls. The old light house will help you give an end-of-the-world atmosphere to your pictures.

Penguin Island Rock Hoppers

6.2.4.2 Deseado Bay tour **

3-hour boat-tour visiting a sea-lion rocky island, a Magellanic penguin colony, different cormorant species, dolphins as well as a very interesting coast dominated by Tower rock (in Spanish Piedra Toba), which appears in old drawings

6.2.4.3 Campamento Darwin / Darwin's Camp site ***

80 km from Deseado there is a ranch that offers a visit to the amazing Deseado's inlet where Darwin camped in 1833. The visit also includes old aboriginal rock paintings and steppe wildlife. When going there, plan to sleep there, stay a full day.

6.2.4.4 Other

Railway Station Museum, Swift Museum and Cabo (cape) Blanco.

6.3 Cape Horn & Fuegian Channels ✳✳✳

The only way to visit this amazing area is by taking the small (aprox 250 pax) cruise ship Cruceros Australis. There are 2 alternatives: Punta Arenas (Chile) to Ushuaia (Argentina) or the opposite direction. The trip lasts 4 days visiting sites only reachable by this ship: glaciers, penguin colonies, elephant seals, long and narrow fjords, historical sites like Woollya and the infamous Cape Horn among many other beauties. If you have time and budget, you must take it, you definitely won't regret it. Fares are high so try to avoid the very high season of January and February.

Fuegian channels – Pia Glacier

6.4 Punta Arenas *

The main city in southern Patagonia does not have so much to do/see but, since it has an airport and a busy harbor you might be arriving or leaving from there, in which case you should spare some time to visit it and its surroundings. Main attractions/activities are:

6.4.1 City tour **

The town holds some impressive old houses from the glory days before the Panama Canal was built. Pay a visit to the Braun Menendez Museum and Sara Braun's house on the main square. Also quite interesting are the Salesian museum and *Nao Victoria* museum, which exhibits true size replicas of famous ships like Magellan's *Nao Victoria* and Darwin's *HMS Beagle*.

6.4.2 Magdalena Island **

An interesting island in the Straits of Magellan, home to a large Magellanic penguin colony and other sea birds.

6.4.3 The King penguin colony in Useless Bay *

A full day tour across the Straits of Magellan to see this iconic penguin.

Punta Arenas

6.5 Patagonian Epic Roads***

Two iconic roads run along the Andes on both countries for hundreds of kilometers. Although there are less than 100 km between them, the environments they cross couldn't be more different. Both roads demand a lot of driving. If planning to rent a car keep in mind that drop off in a different city is not allowed neither in Chile nor in Argentina. Motorhomes or campers are rare, so you'll have to sleep in small hotels in villages except in a couple of cities along the road.

6.5.1 Route 40 (Argentina) ***

From San Martín de los Andes to El Calafate there are 1600 km, plan no less than 10 days. Some great things to see are obvious but others mean getting off the beaten track through dust roads. If you're renting a car you'll have to return where you've started so there are two alternative ways back: Carretera Austral or Patagonian coast (Route 3). In any case plan at least 3 weeks for the grand tour.

6.5.2 Carretera Austral (Chile) ***

The extremes of this road are Caleta Gonzalo and O'Higgins, separated 1000 km away. Since the road is not connected by land with the rest of Chile you can reach the north by ferry from Puerto Montt or from Argentina across the Andes. Since you must return to where the car was rented, we suggest a couple of alternatives.

6.5.2.1 Short Alternative in Chile
Start in Puerto Montt take a ferry to Chaiten (or to Chiloé and then another one to Chaiten) and drive Carretera Austral until Puerto Chacabuco and there take the Navimag ferry back to Puerto Montt.

6.5.2.2 Short Alternative through Argentina
Start in Puerto Montt take a ferry to Chaiten (or to Chiloe and then another one to Chaiten) and drive Carretera Austral until Yelcho, cross the border to Argentina and take Route 40 north to Bariloche and Puerto Montt.

6.5.2.3 Long Alternative

Start in Puerto Montt take a ferry to Chaiten (or to Chiloe and then another one to Chaiten) and drive Carretera Austral until Puerto Bertrand and cross the border to Argentina with 2 further alternatives

Take Route 40 north to Bariloche and Puerto Montt

Take Route 40 south to Calafate, Torres del Paine and in Puerto Natales take Navimag back to Puerto Montt.

6.6 Northwestern Patagonia ***

A long guide can be written about this region but it is seldom visited by travelers from the northern hemisphere. Even though there are literally more than a hundred interesting things to see and do here there is no iconic and spectacular place. Another issue to keep in mind about this region is that many-many people come from Buenos Aires and other cities so places can be crowded, weakening your experience there. Avoid travelling in January or February. Main places to visit are: San Martín de los Andes, Villa la Angostura, Bariloche, Puerto Varas, Chiloé.

Hotel Correntoso – Villa la Angostura

6.7 Chilean channels**

The Patagonian Pacific coast is a maze of channels and fjords similar to the Fuegian channels. Ships can navigate hundreds of kilometers without coming out to open sea. The islands are covered by rain forest and many fjords have glaciers coming down from the Andean ice fields. Some of the channels can be seen and enjoyed while driving the Carretera Austral but there are also two navigation alternatives that must be mentioned.

6.7.1 Skorpios Cruise ***

This is a one-week cruise leaving from Puerto Montt and sailing south into the maze of channels. The jewel of the trip is the glacier San Rafael near which the zodiacs will float among icebergs.

6.7.2 Navimag *

This is a three-day ferry going from Puerto Natales to Puerto Montt (with a mid-stop at Puerto Chacabuco) and back. Even though its main purpose is not tourism the trip is definitely outstanding.

6.8 Other Activities

6.8.1 Fly fishing and hunting

Many travelers come to Patagonia from overseas specifically to fish or hunt. Most usually their trip is one week long and does not involve any other activity.

6.8.1.1 Fishing

Trouts were introduced in Patagonia by the end of the 1800s and they now inhabit most of the mountain rivers and lakes. Gradually fly-fishing begun to attract fans from the northern hemisphere and some fishing lodges became world famous (like Maria Behety in Tierra del Fuego). Fishing is also possible for tourists who want to spend a half a day in this activity. Most of the towns have fishing guides that also rent the necessary equipment.

6.8.1.2 Hunting

Red deer and wild boars were introduced in northern Patagonia in the beginning of the 20th century. Today many Estancias (ranches) have hunting lodges, mostly for foreigners.

6.8.2 Skiing

Patagonia has a great number of sky resorts. Keep in mind that skiing season goes from June to September except in Ushuaia, where it goes up to October. The main ski resorts are: Cerro Catedral/Bariloche – Chapelco/San Martín de los Andes – Cerro Bayo/La Angostura – La Hoya/Esquel – Cerro Castor/Ushuaia.

6.8.3 Scuba diving

This sport is performed almost all along the Patagonian coast but only a few places offer it as a service for tourists with little or no experience: Puerto Madryn, Puerto Pirámides, Puerto Deseado and Ushuaia.

6.8.4 Golf

Although there are golf facilities in places like Bariloche, San Martín de los Andes and Cholila they are only open for members.

If you are interested there is the possibility, if writing in advance, of receiving an invitation.

6.8.5 Photography

Landscapes, animals, flowers, activities and even heritage can all be attractive for your social networks. We have recently published a guide with the best places, situations and tips for great travel-photography using only a smart phone or pocket camera.

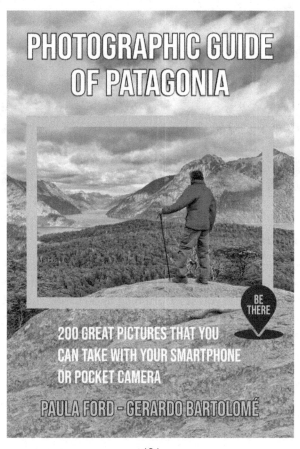

Chapter 7
Ideas & Combinations

7.1 Introduction

Sometimes it is difficult to start planning a trip. There are so many alternatives! To help you, we give some alternatives that sound logical to us, so that you start planning by adjusting the one that suits you best. All of these alternatives go from November to March except the last one that focuses on whale watching.

7.2 Two weeks (including travel days)

It's a bit tight but, maybe that's the best that you can do!

7.2.1 Alternative only Argentina

Schedule is tight so you better stick to visiting the Argentina side: Buenos Aires 2 days – El Calafate 2 days – El Chaltén 2 days – Ushuaia 3 days – all expressed in full days + 3 mixed travelling days in between + 2 travelling days from/to overseas, making a total of 14 days.

7.2.2 Alternative with Torres del Paine

Schedule is tight so you choose Torres del Paine over similar El Chaltén: Buenos Aires 2 days – El Calafate 2 days – Torres del Paine 2 days – Ushuaia 3 days – all expressed in full days + 3 mixed travelling days in between + 2 travelling days from/to overseas, making a total of 14 days.

7.3 Three weeks (including travel days)

You can have a great time but you'll still leave some amazing places without visiting, maybe for next time!

7.3.1 Alternative of the Big Four

You have time to see the most important things: Buenos Aires 3 days – El Calafate 3 days – El Chaltén 3 days – Torres del Paine 3 days – Ushuaia 3 days – all expressed in full days + 4 mixed travelling days in between + 2 travelling days from/to overseas, making a total of 21 days.

7.3.2 Alternative Coast and Andes, only Argentina

This alternative is for those who love wildlife, but you must leave behind the scenic landscape of Torres del Paine: Buenos Aires 3 days – Valdes Peninsula or Bahía Bustamante 3 days – Ushuaia 3

days – El Calafate 3 days – El Chaltén 3 days – all expressed in full days + 4 mixed travelling days in between + 2 travelling days from/ to overseas, making a total of 21 days.

7.3.3 Alternative Mostly Chile

In this alternative you're leaving behind some important places but travelling will be more comfortable (and expensive): Santiago 2 days – Torres del Paine 3 days – Fuegian channels 4 days – Ushuaia 4 days – Buenos Aires 2 days + 4 mixed travelling days in between + 2 travelling days from/to overseas, making a total of 21 days.

7.4 Four weeks (including travel days)

You can have a great time and will need an important budget.

7.4.1 Alternative Grand Tour

Comfortable travelling and time to enjoy incredible places -
Santiago 2 days – Torres del Paine 3 days – Fuegian channels 4
days – Ushuaia 3 days – El Calafate 3 days – El Chaltén 3 days –
Buenos Aires 3 days + 5 mixed travelling days in between + 2
travelling days from/to overseas, making a total of 28 days.

7.4.2 Alternative Coast and Andes mainly Argentina

For those who love wildlife, scenic landscapes and comfort:
Buenos Aires 4 days – Valdes Peninsula or Bahía Bustamante or
Puerto Deseado 3 days – Ushuaia 4 days – El Chaltén 4 days –
Torres del Paine 3 days – El Calafate 3 days – all expressed in full
days + 5 mixed travelling days in between + 2 travelling days from/
to overseas, making a total of 28 days.

7.5 Winter week for Whale watching

During July or August when the number of whales hits its' maximum. Buenos Aires 2 days – Pto Piramides 2 days – Pto Madryn/Gaiman/Trelew 2 days + 1 day for internal travelling + 2 days for overseas travelling, making a total of 9 days.

Whale watching

Chapter 8
The Authors

Paula and Gerardo have been travelling through Patagonia for more than thirty years.

Paula Ford was born in Buenos Aires and is married to Gerardo Bartolomé. As a Biologist and member of the Conicet (the scientific research council of Argentina) she is the author of many scientific papers.

Gerardo Bartolomé was also born in Buenos Aires. After working many years as an Engineer, in 2005 he wrote his first historical novel "Darwin's Betrayal" and since then he has written many other books. In 2018 he founded Ediciones Históricas, a publishing company dedicated to history and travelling.

Both, Paula and Gerardo published, in 2016, "Patagonia: A Voyage to its Enigmas" (third edition, now) where Paula's photos give life to Gerardo's writings about eleven iconic places of this region.

They now want to share their knowledge and experience with all those who plan to visit this wild and fascinating land.

Soon Paula and Gerardo will publish two interesting books. A) A Photography guide of Patagonia so that everyone can take and share great pictures, and also B) "History of Patagonia".

Feel free to write to them for further information or doubts that you might have. Their email is Consultas@EdicionesHistoricas.com.ar.

Made in the USA
Las Vegas, NV
21 January 2024

84711387R00075